Drug Edu

Series Advisers

Gerald Haigh   Writer and Consultant in Education

Pauline Maskell   Secondary Head of Health Studies

John Sutton   General Secretary, Secondary Heads Association

Advisory Panel

Ruth Joyce   Adviser on Drugs and Health Education

Mike Kirby   Writer on Education

Terry Saunders   Secondary Head of Biology

Anne Morgan   Primary Deputy Headteacher

Elaine Wilson   Secondary Head of Science

2nd edition

ISBN: 1 85467 324 6

© 1995

Daniels Publishing
38 Cambridge Place
Cambridge CB2 1NS
Tel: 01223 467144 Fax: 01223 467145

Foreword

I like the idea of Quick Guides. Teachers need reliable information and advice on a very wide range of subjects related to their work and they need it to be accessible and concise. This series attempts to meet those needs by drawing on the knowledge of experienced practitioners and presenting the essential material in a format which facilitates rapid reference and provides valuable action checklists.

I am sure that these guides will be useful to teachers, to governors, to parents and indeed to all who are concerned with the effective management of all aspects of education.

John Sutton
General Secretary
Secondary Heads Association

Drug Education, ages 11–18: a quick guide

About the author

Janice Slough is a consultant and trainer in Personal and Social Education. She is based on the Isle of Wight and has previously worked as a teacher, youth worker and health education co-ordinator.

Drug Education, ages 11–18: a quick guide

Contents

Contents (continued)

Introduction

Drug misuse among young people has increased rapidly in this country in recent years, causing widespread concern. Parents are worried that their children will be influenced and their communities will suffer from the effects of drug-related crime. Schools have been told that the government intends to monitor their policy for drug education and the management of drug-related incidents on school premises as part of the regular programme of inspections by the Office of Standards in Education (OFSTED).

Drug education is therefore an important part of the secondary school curriculum. It is our task in education to equip our students to live in a drug-orientated society, where drugs and similar substances are used medically and socially, legally and illegally, and the same drug can cure or destroy, depending who uses it and how it is used. The young people we teach need help to make informed and healthy choices about drug use.

This publication is intended to guide schools through the steps for planning and implementing a comprehensive drug education programme. It also suggests ways in which parents, governors and interested people from the community can be involved in a partnership to develop a whole school policy, including guidelines for coping with drug misuse. Each step provides aims, ideas and information, to help schools explore the issues and implications they will have to address in order to achieve a positive and relevant response to drugs.

Why drug education is important

- Drugs are an important part of modern life; many people need them to improve the quality of their lives and to eliminate disease and pain.

- Television, films and advertising can convey a sophisticated, exciting image of inappropriate or social drug use.

- Alcohol and nicotine are still the most widely available and abused drugs, and cause much physical and social harm. They are also the drugs that young people are most likely to experiment with.

- Young people are often caught up with the drugs that go with fashion and youth culture. Social life and drug taking can become synonymous, as with raves and Ecstasy.

- Adolescence is a time of uncertainty and change, leaving young people vulnerable to peer pressure, lacking confidence and wanting to rebel and experiment. These factors can lead to the misuse of drugs.

- Drug education can be a vehicle for addressing myths and misconceptions about drugs and drug taking.

- Young people need helped to equip themselves with the skills they need to cope with a drug-orientated society. The development of self esteem, which is a major part of drug education, helps them to maintain a healthy attitude towards drugs.

- The illicit drug trade continues to grow and the misuse of drugs has become a serious problem in many countries.

Influences on young people

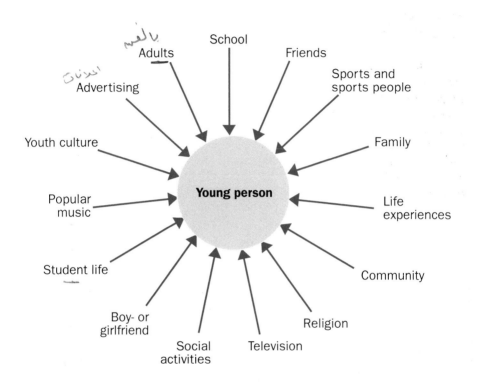

'A drug is a substance that alters the way in which the body functions.' Martin Plant, **Drugs in Perspective.**

☐ The word 'drug' covers anything taken into the body to change the way it functions. It includes medicines, alcohol and tobacco as well as illegal drugs such as heroin or cannabis.

☐ Some drugs have only a physical effect on the body, such as relieving pain or fighting infection.

☐ Others have a psychological effect as well, in that they affect the mind or emotions.

☐ Many drugs which are used medically for their physical effects also have psychological ones.

☐ Some substances whose main use is not for their effect on the body, such as the solvents in glues, can also be used like drugs.

☐ Sometimes the word 'substance' is used to mean drugs and other materials which can be used like drugs. However, there are many more substances in the world which are not drugs and have no drug-like effects.

Socially acceptable drugs

Caffeine

Caffeine is found in coffee, tea, soft drinks, chocolate and 'over the counter' painkillers. 500–600 milligrams (mg) of caffeine a day can cause feelings of anxiety and restlessness. A regular user of 370 mg (seven or more cups of strong coffee) can experience withdrawal symptoms, including severe headaches. Caffeine, when used in small doses, is pleasant and mildly stimulating.

The drugs that everyone uses aren't necessarily safer than the ones the law forbids.

Alcohol

Alcoholic drinks consist mainly of ethanol, a form of alcohol, and water. Alcohol is a depressant which affects those parts of the brain concerned with pain, self-criticism and self-control. The user can therefore feel relaxed and less anxious. The efficiency of mental and physical controls is reduced, so that emotional reactions can become exaggerated, sometimes leading to risky behaviour, violence or unsafe sex. Excessive drinking of alcohol can cause obesity, social problems and physical damage. In extreme cases it can result in convulsions, coma and death. Young people are more susceptible to the effects of alcohol than adults, and there is an added risk if they combine alcohol with other drugs. Responsible drinking, on the other hand, can be pleasant, relaxing and socially acceptable.

Tobacco is probably the most addictive and most dangerous drug in use today, and smoking remains the largest preventable cause of death. The 1992 Health of the Nation white paper includes a target for reducing smoking among 11–15 year olds.

Nicotine

Tobacco smoke consists of droplets of tar, nicotine, carbon monoxide and other gases. Nicotine stimulates the body by increasing the pulse rate and blood pressure and can alleviate stress and anxiety. It is physically addictive; if a smoker gives up, they can experience anxiety and distressing physical symptoms. Long-term use can result in heart disease, heart attacks, bad circulation, lung cancer, cancer of the mouth and throat, blood clots and ulcers, some of which can be fatal. Tobacco smoking is becoming less socially acceptable, because of the unpleasant effects on other people ('passive smoking').

Drug Education, ages 11–18: a quick guide

Prescribed and 'over the counter' drugs

'Recognise that
Britain is a drug
using society and
recognise the
different patterns
of use and their
effects.'
Curriculum
Guidance 5.

☐ Prescribed drugs, such as Valium (diazepam), can cause problems resulting from prolonged or excessive use. It is illegal to share prescribed drugs with anyone else.

☐ 'Over the counter' drugs, such as cough medicines, can also be misused and cause problems when overused or taken without regard to instructions. These drugs, stolen from chemists' shops or home medicine cabinets, are sold to young people on the streets.

☐ It is important to:
- keep medicines locked away.
- read labels carefully.
- use medicinal drugs only when really necessary (a short walk, for instance, can cure a headache).
- use prescribed drugs as instructed by the doctor or pharmacist.
- throw surplus drugs away safely.

Solvents

'Solvent' is the collective word commonly used to describe a whole range of volatile substances such as the solvents in glues, paints, dry cleaning fluids, degreasing mixtures and nail varnish removers, as well as the propellant gases in aerosols and fire extinguishers, and fuels such as cigarette lighter gas or petrol. In an average home there are usually over 30 such volatile products.

- The effect of inhaling these substances is similar to being drunk on alcohol. Dizziness and euphoria are common and users can experience feelings of unreality, leading to bizarre actions. The effect is quicker than alcohol and wears off quickly, so that users need to keep repeating the process.

- Solvents are used by younger people than other drugs, partly because they are so easily available.

- Sniffing solvents can be fatal, and over 100 people a year die as a result of volatile substance abuse; most of these are young people.

- 'Sudden sniffing death syndrome' occurs when solvents bring on heart failure, often as a result of exertion, such as running away while intoxicated. It is vital therefore that anyone finding sniffers should not chase them, as this could cause a heart attack.

- Accidents are also associated with volatile substance abuse, as users tend to sniff in dangerous places such as canal banks, railway land and derelict buildings.

Illegal drugs

☐ **Cannabis** is the most widely used illegal drug in Britain today. It comes from a bushy plant and is normally found in herbal or resin form. It is generally smoked with tobacco and carries the same risks to health. As well as causing cancer and low fetal weight there is growing evidence that cannabis can cause long term memory loss. It is dangerous to drive or take part activities requiring concentration when under its influence, as it causes changes in perception and judgement. It is not physically addictive but regular users may feel it is an important part of their life. This has been described as 'psychological dependence'.

'Teachers should have up to date factual information about drugs and their effects.' Drug Misuse and the Young: a guide for the education service.

☐ **LSD**: LSD stands for **lysergic acid diethylamide**, an artificially made substance. It can be obtained in tablet form, capsules or absorbed on paper (tabs). Users experience hallucinations, which may make them attempt dangerous activities, possibly leading to accidents, even fatal ones. Death due to the physical effects of the drug is unknown but mental disorders can occur.

☐ **Hallucinogenic mushrooms**: Certain fungi (sometimes called magic mushrooms) have similar effects to LSD. The main dangers are of mistakenly eating a poisonous variety or being involved in accidents while hallucinating.

'Know the basic facts about substances including their effects and relevant legislation.' Curriculum Guidance 5.

☐ **Ecstasy** (**MDMA**) is a stimulant amphetamine derivative (see below) which is hallucinogenic in large doses. If it is taken in a hot atmosphere such as at a rave, the user can suffer heat stroke. High doses can lead to panic attacks, anxiety and insomnia. Long-term use is thought to damage the brain or liver.

☐ **Amphetamines** (**speed**) are stimulants in the form of tablets or powder. Prolonged heavy use can cause heart failure and lead to mental disorders.

☐ **Cocaine** is a stimulant that comes from the coca plant. It can make people feel excited and alert and overcome feelings of pain, fatigue and weakness. However, the effect is short-lived, and depression and insomnia can follow. Sniffing cocaine can cause damage to the nose membranes. **Crack** or freebase cocaine is a smokable form which is rapidly absorbed into the body. It carries a higher risk of addiction.

☐ **Heroin** is derived from opium, from the opium poppy, but some is now produced artificially. The dangers associated with this drug are from dirty needles, infection from sharing needles, impurities, reduced appetite, self-neglect and overdose. It can cause physical dependence and is associated with a chaotic lifestyle.

Drugs used in sport

Anabolic steroids: used by athletes and bodybuilders to increase the bulk of their muscles. The drugs are derived from the male hormone testosterone and can also stimulate aggression. Side effects can include a reduced sex drive and sperm count, acne, liver disease, ulcers and gastrointestinal bleeding.

Beta blockers are used medically to treat heart conditions. They are misused in sports such as snooker to reduce the effects of stress. The misuse of these can result in heart problems and breathing difficulties.

Narcotic analgesics and corticosteroids are groups of drugs that block the sensation of pain and relax the nervous system. Athletes may be tempted to use them in order to train or compete despite an injury. However, there is a real danger of more acute injury happening.

Human chorionic gonadotrophin (HCG): This is a natural human hormone which can be used to stimulate testosterone production and thus boost muscle growth. The International Olympic Committee introduced a new doping class of 'peptide hormones and analogues' in 1989, to combat the use of this type of drug.

Erythropoietin (EPO): This boosts red blood cell production and thus the oxygen-carrying capacity of the blood. It is used for the treatment of anaemia but has been abused to improve the performance of sprinters.

'Recognise that individuals are responsible for choices they make about drug use.' Curriculum Guidance 5.

The law on drugs is complex, but everyone needs to know the basic points.

- Illegal drugs such as cannabis, crack, LSD, cocaine, Ecstasy are covered by the Misuse of Drugs Act. It is illegal to possess, grow, sell or supply them.

- If you find, or think you have found, an illegal drug, you should inform the police and hand over the substance, if possible in front of a witness.

- You can take a substance away from a person in order to prevent them committing an offence. Then you should inform the police and hand over the substance, if possible in front of a witness.

- It is illegal to drive while under the influence of drugs.

- It is an offence for an occupier or manager to knowingly let cannabis be used or supplied on their premises.

- It is illegal to share prescribed drugs with another person.

- It is illegal to sell tobacco products to anyone under the age of 16, but people under that age are not committing an offence if they smoke tobacco.

- It is an offence to supply a young person under the age of 18 with a volatile substance if you believe that it will be used for intoxication.

- Possession of solvents and sniffing are not offences. The police can only intervene if a criminal act results or is likely to result.

☐ People under 14 years old are not allowed in the bar of licensed premises.

☐ A 16-year-old can drink beer, port, cider or perry (or wine in Scotland) if they are having a meal in an area set aside for that purpose.

☐ No alcohol can be sold or delivered to a person under 18 except for consumption with a meal.

☐ 14- to 17-year-olds are allowed on licensed premises but cannot drink or buy alcohol or be employed in a public house.

☐ It is illegal to drive, or try to drive, with more than 35 microgrammes of alcohol in 100 millilitres of breath.

☐ Advertisements for alcoholic drinks should not be directed at young people under 18 or suggest
  • that the product advertised helps people to gain social acceptance.
  • that it is desirable to drink products high in alcohol.
  • that heavy drinking is admirable or amusing or enhances personal relationships.

☐ Amyl nitrite (liquid gold or poppers): This is not illegal to sell or use, and is often available in joke or sex shops.

☐ Hallucinogenic mushrooms (magic mushrooms): It is legal to possess them in their natural state but once they are processed they are illegal.

'Good links between the police and the education service can give students a better understanding of, and a greater respect for, the law and the need for its enforcement.' **Drug Misuse and the Young: a guide for the education service.**

If someone is ill, don't panic, but get help at once.

If you find someone who appears seriously intoxicated, or is unconscious or semi-conscious:

☐ Call an ambulance immediately and summon any medical or nursing professionals who may be available, or a first-aider.

☐ Make sure the person is not in danger of hurting themselves.

☐ Make sure they can breathe: clear the mouth of obstructions and pull the tongue forward if necessary.

☐ Loosen clothing around their neck.

☐ Place the person in the recovery position: lie them on their side, with the top leg bent slightly in front of them to stop them rolling forward. The lower arm should also be bent up in front of them. The head should be tilted well back with the top hand underneath to support it.

☐ If the person is not breathing, or if their face, lips or tongue turn blue, they should be resuscitated immediately by a trained person.

☐ If it is a student, their parents should be informed.

☐ Keep any tablets or other substances you find, or samples of the vomit if the person has been sick. Knowing what they have taken could save their life, so make sure the samples go with them to the hospital.

Action plan for implementing drug education in secondary schools

□ Step one: Initial consultation

Target: A shared understanding of the aims of drug education and of what the school and community want to achieve for its students

□ Step two: Policy development

Target: A written policy on a whole school approach to drugs and drug education

□ Step three: Planning for the curriculum

Target: A clear idea of what we want to achieve through the drug education curriculum

□ Step four: Drug education strategies

Target: Agreement on a shared approach and methodology

□ Step five: Content of the curriculum

Target: The production of a drug education curriculum framework

'A planned programme of health education is one of the ways in which schools prepare students for the opportunities, responsibilities and experiences of adult life.' **Curriculum Guidance 5.**

Planning questionnaire

The more we know before beginning to plan, the more effective the resulting programme will be.

- [ ] What do we mean by 'drugs'?
- [ ] What are our concerns?
- [ ] What are our students' needs and perceptions?
- [ ] What are the drug issues in the community?
- [ ] What drugs and substances are our students already familiar with?
- [ ] What do we want to achieve?
- [ ] What policies will we need to discuss and develop?
- [ ] Why do we want to address drugs and drug education in the curriculum?
- [ ] What messages do we want to put across?
- [ ] What is already happening regarding drug education in the curriculum?
- [ ] Who will co-ordinate the programme?
- [ ] What is the best context for a drug education programme?
- [ ] How do we plan a comprehensive drug education programme?
- [ ] Who do we involve in the planning?
- [ ] What resources and skills do we already have available in the school?
- [ ] What other help is available from outside?
- [ ] Is drug education in the school development plan?
- [ ] How can we involve parents and governors?
- [ ] What staff training will be necessary?
- [ ] What resources will we need?
- [ ] How much finance have we available for this programme?
- [ ] What do we want the programme to look like?
- [ ] How can we assess the effectiveness of the programme?

Step one: Initial consultation

Target: A shared understanding of the aims of drug education and what the school wants to achieve for its students.

Possible ways to go about this:

☐ Identify a member of staff to be the drug education co-ordinator.

☐ Circulate a discussion paper to staff, governors and parents.

☐ Hold a governors' meeting to discuss
- the need for drug education
- aims
- expectations
- rationale
- concerns

☐ Staff meeting.

☐ Parents' meeting.

☐ Contact people who may be able to help with training and advice, such as the LEA Health Education Adviser, youth workers, Drug Prevention Team and Health Promotion Unit or Service.

Drug education should be a partnership between the student, school, home and community.

Knowing what messages we want to put across is the basis of a good drug education programme.

☐ There is no such thing as a safe drug.

☐ Alcohol can be pleasurable if used responsibly and safely, but it is a dangerous drug.

☐ The effects of any drug will depend on the user, the situation, and the circumstances surrounding the user.

☐ The same drug can have different effects at different times.

☐ The effects of drugs can reduce responsibility for safe sex and other appropriate behaviour, and increase the risk of accidents.

☐ Friends are the drug-pushers young people are most likely to encounter.

☐ Any drug, legal or illegal, prescribed or 'over the counter', can be misused and is potentially harmful.

☐ Learn to deal with stress, don't try to hide it.

☐ Taking drugs does not solve problems or bring more than temporary happiness.

☐ Do what you feel is good for you: don't be pressurised into doing anything you don't want to, or that makes you feel uneasy.

A drug awareness programme for adults

Purpose

- To increase knowledge and awareness of the different kinds of drugs available and how they are used.
- To raise awareness of our attitudes and values concerning drugs and drug issues.
- To explore ways of dealing with drug misuse.
- To find out what other agencies are doing.

Content

- Definition of a drug.
- The local picture of drug use.
- Facts about drugs.
- Use and misuse of drugs.
- Effects of drugs.
- Attitudes and values about drug use.
- Why people take drugs.
- Signs and symptoms of drug use.
- Defining a drug problem.
- Drugs and the law.
- Dealing with drug use.
- Local and national agencies that provide help and information services.

'An appropriate level of training, information and guidance needs to be provided not only to the teaching staff delivering drug education but also to all other teaching and non teaching staff involved in the school community.' **Drug Education in Schools: the need for a new impetus.**

'The involvement of parents is an important factor in ensuring the effectiveness of any messages about drug education.'
Drug Education in Schools: the need for a new impetus.

'Drugs and our Young People'

Purpose

☐ To understand more about the world of drugs and drug taking.

☐ To share common concerns and strategies in working with young people.

☐ To establish a partnership between home and school for the health and well being of our young people.

Programme

☐ Welcome and introduction to the evening.

☐ Background to drugs and drug taking: influences, pressures and trends, locally and nationally.

☐ Drugs:
   • facts and information.
   • individual drugs and their effects.
   • drug legislation.

☐ How can we help our young people?
   • needs, wants, skills, values.
   • sharing experiences.

☐ Dealing with drug-related incidents:
   • situations and guidelines.
   • signs and symptoms.
   • where to get help.

☐ Summary and evaluation:
   • Where do we go from here?

Step two: Policy development

Target: A written policy on a whole school approach to drugs and drug issues.

Possible ways to go about this:

☐ Set up a drugs policy working group.

☐ Develop the concept of a Health Promoting School (see Goals for a Health Promoting School).

☐ Work towards a Healthy School Award (details available from your LEA Health Education Co-ordinator or Health Promotion Unit).

☐ Develop a smoke-free school policy.

☐ Produce guidelines for dealing with:
  • sensitive issues.
  • pastoral work and confidentiality.
  • misuse of drugs by students.
  • notification of drug use, and follow-up.
  • the discovery of substances on school premises.
  • drug education in the curriculum.
  • the use of social and medical drugs on school premises.

☐ Explore a whole school approach to developing students' self-esteem and confidence.

How can we achieve a whole school approach to drugs and drug issues?

Specimen drugs policy for a secondary school

You cannot buy a drugs policy off the peg; it needs to be tailored to your own school, community and circumstances.

- The school does not condone the use of legal or illegal substances on school premises, but our policy is to put the young person's welfare first.
- Students found smoking in school are counselled by form tutors or heads of house. Parents are informed, and further discussion may be necessary.
- Alcohol may not be brought into school. Students who come to school drunk also receive counselling, and parents are informed.
- Signs of misuse of other substances are easily confused with other problems. It is important not to jump to conclusions, but to discuss students' problems sympathetically. Find out the extent of the problem, explain the limits of confidentiality and establish what help the student needs.
- A teacher suspecting drug use should discuss this with the parents.
- If there is evidence that a student is using drugs, the teacher must inform the head teacher, who will contact the parents.
- If it seems that illegal substances are being brought into school, the school can discuss this with the community police liaison officer.
- If illegal substances are found, a designated member of staff will destroy them or pass them on to the police to prevent an offence being committed.
- The police will be informed if illegal drugs are used or sold in school.
- First offenders are most likely to receive an informal warning, which does not establish a criminal record.

(Adapted by kind permission of Hinchingbrooke School, Huntingdon.)

Guidelines on incidents involving drugs

If a student is found with a misusable substance:

- ☐ It should be taken away from him or her and locked away, if possible in the presence of a witness.

- ☐ Decide whether to destroy the substance or, if it is an illegal substance, consult the police.

- ☐ Interview the student or students separately.

- ☐ Notify their parents.

- ☐ Develop an action plan in consultation with the student, parents and relevant staff, for medical help, counselling, discipline, coping strategies or education, as appropriate.

- ☐ Punitive action, especially exclusion from school, against student drug users could be counterproductive, benefiting neither:
  - the school: excluding students could make drug use appear glamorous and exciting to other students, as well as creating unease and suspicion amongst staff and students.
  - the student: if alienated, the student may become further involved and problems with their schooling may be exacerbated.

- ☐ The behaviour, not the person, should be seen as unacceptable. The negative influence that a drug user might have on other students should be considered and strategies established to minimise the risk.

'Alternatives to permanent exclusion/ expulsion should be preferred where possible.' **Drug Education in Schools: the need for a new impetus.**

Guidelines on suspected drug problems among students

The school can play an important part in helping young people overcome any problems they may have with drugs.

If you are concerned that a student may be having problems due to drug use:

☐ Observe the student's behaviour.

☐ Share your concerns with colleagues or the head teacher.

☐ Record your concerns and observations in writing:
- conversations with the student.
- changes in behaviour.
- physical and emotional signs of possible drug use.
- friendships.
- comments from other adults or students.

☐ If your suspicions are confirmed, consult:
- the head teacher and other members of staff.
- your educational welfare officer.
- the student.
- other agencies such as a Drug Prevention Unit.
- the student's family.

☐ Assess the situation and draw up an appropriate action plan with the student.

☐ Help the student put the plan into action.

☐ Review the situation regularly until there is no longer a problem.

Guidelines on confidentiality

- It is not realistic to guarantee complete confidentiality for a student who may have problems with drugs.

- The student should always be told what information is going to be passed on, and to whom.

- If teachers suspect a student is having drug problems, they will usually consult the student's parents and other staff who know the student.

- If there is a risk of harm to the student or other people, teachers are obliged to inform the head teacher or other colleagues.

- If the law is being broken, the police normally have to be told.

- If a student becomes ill, medical or nursing staff need to know about all factors that may be relevant, including any suspicions of drug taking.

- There is rarely any need to disclose the details of students' personal problems to other people, and this should never happen without the student's permission.

'In monitoring incidents, care should be taken to ensure confidentiality.' **Drug Education in Schools: the need for a new impetus.**

The goals for a Health Promoting School, or a Healthy School Award, are the same that any school concerned for its students' welfare should aim for.

☐ A school ethos which promotes equal opportunity, genuine care and concern for others, shared responsibility, and partnership.

☐ An environment which is stimulating, clean, tidy and safe.

☐ A health education curriculum which is co-ordinated, planned and progressive, and is integrated into the school development plan.

☐ Classroom methodology which emphasises student-centred activities and a participatory approach.

☐ A health promoting workplace for staff and students alike, with emphasis on being safe, building good relationships, reducing stress, taking exercise, eliminating heart disease and promoting self-esteem.

☐ Strong links with the local community.

☐ Planned development of personal and social skills.

☐ A strong pastoral system built around designated individuals with appropriate skills, such as counselling.

☐ An efficient and easily understood communication system.

☐ Appropriate policies for:
- drug education.
- dealing with drug related incidents.
- the use of alcohol and tobacco on the premises.
- bullying.
- child protection.
- equal opportunities.
- healthy eating.
- sex education.

Example of a school smoking policy

Rationale: Tobacco smoking is the cause of much ill health and death among both smokers and passive smokers (those who breathe other people's smoke). It is therefore an important health and safety issue for everyone who uses our school. Everyone has a right to breathe clean air and adults have a responsibility to see that young people enjoy this right and can look to positive non-smoking adult models within the school.

The ultimate aim is to create a non-smoking school community, but this must be achieved in co-operation with the members of the school, not by coercion.

Aims

- ☐ To provide a smoke free environment for students.
- ☐ To guarantee non-smokers the right to work in a smoke-free environment, while recognising the needs of any staff who smoke.
- ☐ To encourage, help and support staff and students who want to give up smoking.
- ☐ To help staff and students not to start using tobacco.

Implementation

- ☐ Smoking is not allowed on school premises, including the school grounds (if schools wish to designate a smoking area, it should be somewhere not used by students, such as a small room off the staff room). Students are not allowed to smoke.
- ☐ Smoking is not allowed at any evening function; this must be agreed when parts of the buildings are hired out.
- ☐ All potential new members of staff should be informed of the policy and agree to abide by it.
- ☐ Visitors should be informed of the policy when they arrive. Clear signs should also be displayed around the school.
- ☐ Help will be provided for any student or member of staff who wishes to give up smoking, in consultation with the school nurse and health promotion workers.
- ☐ The school policy on smoking will be reinforced by special promotion at parents' evenings and on occasions like National No Smoking Day.

The drug education curriculum must be based on a clear understanding of what the school can and should hope to achieve.

Target:

A clear idea of what we want to achieve through drug education.

Possible ways to go about this:

☐ Set up a working party to produce a framework for drug education, containing the entitlement to knowledge, skills and values of each student.

☐ Organise a curriculum audit to ascertain what is already being covered in various subjects and years.

The aims of the drug education curriculum in secondary schools

'The essential aim should be to give pupils the facts, emphasise the benefits of a healthy lifestyle and give young people the knowledge and skills to make informed and responsible choices now and later in life.' *Drug Prevention and Schools.*

In more detail, the aims of secondary school drug education should be to:

The school should decide what it wants to achieve in relation to both the general aims of drug education and its own particular needs and circumstances.

- ☐ Encourage a healthy respect for all substances taken into the body.

- ☐ Raise students' awareness of the world of drugs so that they can make informed, responsible and healthy choices.

- ☐ Encourage positive attitudes towards healthy living and lifestyles.

- ☐ Promote a non-smoking lifestyle among young people.

- ☐ Develop an understanding of the dangers of injecting drugs, particularly HIV infection.

- ☐ Introduce students to alternative activities and interests that focus on their successes.

- ☐ Help them understand and cope with the pressures and influences that may lead to the misuse of drugs.

- ☐ Enable each student to develop confidence and self-esteem.

- ☐ Develop an awareness of responsibility for themselves and each other.

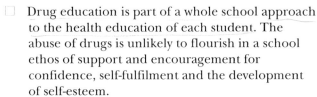

The wide range of issues involved in drug education means that those delivering it need to be especially well informed.

- Drug education is part of a whole school approach to the health education of each student. The abuse of drugs is unlikely to flourish in a school ethos of support and encouragement for confidence, self-fulfilment and the development of self-esteem.

- Drug education concerns both legal and illegal drugs, and those taken socially or used as medicines, whether on prescription or bought 'over the counter'. It should also include substances such as solvents, plants and fungi which can be used for their drug-like effects, even though that is not their main use.

- The focus should be on the person who is taking or might be taking the drugs rather than on the drugs themselves.

- Drug education can never be accomplished by a 'one-off' course. It should be planned and progressive, within the broad context of health education.

- When planning drug education, the following factors should be taken into consideration:
  - the maturity of the students.
  - students' needs.
  - community issues and concerns.
  - religious and cultural factors.
  - the expertise of the staff.

- Students need the knowledge to make informed choices, skills to help them resist negative pressures and develop positive lifestyles, and values that encourage respect for themselves and others. Drug education is about the acquisition of knowledge, the development of skills and the exploration of attitudes and values.

A drug education training programme for staff and governors

Purpose

☐ To provide the common base of knowledge, expertise and confidence needed to deliver drug education.

☐ To discuss aims, principles and messages for drug education.

☐ To explore the effectiveness of drug education.

☐ To disseminate appropriate resources.

☐ To plan work for the curriculum.

☐ To explore the school's and individual teacher's responsibility and role in given situations.

'Teachers delivering drug education need to have the confidence to deliver consistent and clear messages about drugs.' Drug Education in Schools: the need for a new impetus.

Content

☐ The needs of our students.

☐ Rationale, aims and principles of drug education.

☐ What messages do we want to put across?

☐ Different approaches to drug education.

☐ The National Curriculum and drug education.

☐ Where should drug education be included in the curriculum?

☐ Resources and materials.

☐ Planning a programme.

☐ Sensitive issues.

All adults concerned with drug education need to approach it consistently, but they should use as much variety in methods as possible.

Target: Agreement on a shared approach and methodology.

Possible ways to go about this:

- [ ] Staff training and discussion on:
  - drug education and the school community.
  - drug education and the school curriculum.
  - different approaches to drug education.
  - a whole school approach to developing self-esteem.
  - a methodology for developing skills and exploring attitudes in the classroom.
  - dealing with sensitive issues.

- [ ] Address drug education in personal and social education with tutors.

- [ ] Drug education can be included in special 'bolt on' projects such as health week, or drama productions.

Approaches to drug education

☐ As students vary, so does their reaction to drug education. Schools should therefore use a variety of teaching approaches, progressing through the school and reinforcing previous learning. 'The best programmes combine several approaches and should contain material on peer influences and refusal skills.' *Reginald Smart, 'Window of Opportunity' Congress, Australia 1991.*

> *It is important that the message is put across in a way that interests students.*

☐ The 'shock horror' approach can be tempting as it is quick, didactic and can be entertaining for the students. However, except in very rare cases, it only has short-term effects: 'However well intentioned, attempts to shock or frighten young people rarely contribute to the development of positive attitudes and behaviours in the long term.' *Curriculum Guidance 5.*

☐ Information alone is unlikely to encourage healthy behaviour. Skills-based lessons, where students participate in making decisions and solving problems, negotiate with each other and practise situations, are essential in changing behaviour and developing values. 'It is widely recognised that the provision and acquisition of information alone is unlikely to promote healthy or discourage unhealthy behaviour.' *Curriculum Guidance 5.*

☐ Participatory methods, such as the use of audio visual aids, visits, games, case-studies, drama, art, surveys and questionnaires, can provide variety and interest in developing the student's understanding and learning.

☐ A judgemental attitude from a teacher may not allow the students to formulate their own opinions, and could suffocate a learning atmosphere.

Sensitive issues that may arise in drug education

Teachers may be worried that they are telling some students things they know only too well already.

☐ Students may already be drinking or smoking regularly and may or may not be old enough to do so legally.

☐ Significant adults in their lives may be smoking.

☐ People at home may misuse drugs.

☐ Students may come under the influence of friends and older young people.

☐ Students may identify with drug-using subcultures.

☐ Students may have problems at home, causing rebellion, loneliness, frustration or sadness.

☐ There may be pressures at school, causing stress or feelings of failure or inadequacy.

☐ The school may come under pressure to sensationalise the issue of drugs with a 'shock horror' approach, in an attempt to frighten young people off drugs.

☐ Adults may be using alcohol or tobacco on the school premises.

☐ Students may be misusing drugs or substances on the school premises.

☐ Students may disclose knowledge of drug misuse, either their own or other people's.

How to deal with sensitive issues in the classroom

Students who drink and smoke regularly: These students must be made well aware that smoking and drinking are not allowed on school premises and that it is school policy to enforce this. They should also be aware that support is available to help them give up and to deal with any problems underlying their use of alcohol or tobacco. Schools may want to investigate local retailers to find out where under-age students may be getting cigarettes and drink, and enlist their help and that of parents and the wider community. It must also be recognised that no law is broken when students aged 16 and over buy and smoke cigarettes, and that those aged 18 and over are legally adult and entitled to drink alcohol.

Teachers will need to strike a balance between concern for their students' welfare and appearing censorious and out of touch.

Misuse of drugs at home: The behaviour of parents who misuse alcohol or illegal drugs will inevitably affect their children. If the school knows this is happening, it should monitor the situation and if necessary consult with professionals in education welfare and child protection.

Students who are under the negative influence of friends and other young people: The school's health education programme should cover strategies for dealing with peer pressure. If schools know there are negative influences affecting their students, this should be tackled promptly in consultation with the student, parents and other professionals.

All issues concerning drug use and problems need to be approached sensitively.

☐ **Pressures at school causing stress or feelings of failure and inadequacy.** Schools should work towards a health promoting environment that provides strategies for the development of students' self-esteem and a pastoral system that allows students to feel confident about approaching teachers with personal concerns. Skills such as managing time and study and dealing with stress and pressure should be part of the personal and social education curriculum.

☐ **Pressure to sensationalise the issue of drugs with a 'shock horror' approach, to frighten young people off drugs.** This type of approach is known to be ineffective except in the very short term. Schools can be pressurised by well meaning groups or individuals to take such a simplistic approach and may be tempted to respond with evidence that 'something is being done', for instance by bringing in an ex-drug user to give a talk. However, effective drug education is a long-term undertaking involving thorough investigation of the issues. Information evenings for parents and other interested adults can be used to explain the school's position on this.

☐ **Students who disclose knowledge about drug misuse, either their own or other people's, in class discussion.** Before encouraging discussion, the teacher should explain the school's policy on confidentiality, and especially make the point that any information about risks to anyone's safety or possible illegal actions will have to be passed on.

Using outside expertise

Many organisations and individuals, both nationally and locally, are concerned about drug misuse . Many of them see preventive education, especially in schools, as a vital way of stemming the tide of illicit drug use. Schools are often approached by people who offer to contribute to drug education: health visitors, health education or promotion officers, drug prevention teams, police officers, ex-users or representatives of religious organisations. If their help is taken up it is important to see them as part, and not all, of the school's drug education programme, and to make sure that their philosophy and materials are in line with the school's approach to drug education.

'Schools need to be aware of the range of agencies and services in their area, including primary healthcare services, which can help in developing the school drug education programme.' **Drug Education in Schools: the need for a new impetus.**

The school should ask the following questions:

- What is the purpose of the visit and what results are expected?

- What will be included in the session?

- How will the visit fit into the whole drug education curriculum?

- What will the content and approach of the materials be in relation to the students' maturity, needs and experience?

- What can the visitor offer that cannot be provided by the school?

- What other schools have received these visits and how have they felt about the effectiveness of the session?

Some schools have invited former drug users to speak to their students. 'In considering such contributions, however, schools should be particularly aware that without sensitive handling, they may perversely serve to glamourise drug misuse and actually encourage experimentation, since the former user is living proof that recovery is possible.' *Drug Misuse and the Young.*

When visiting speakers are involved, their contribution must be planned as part of the overall teaching programme. Teachers should be present when visitors are speaking to the students, so that they know what is said and can deal with any follow-up questions or concerns.

Visiting speakers can offer
- different experiences.
- specialised knowledge.
- a change of face and perspective.
- no preconceived ideas about individual students.
- a support system for school staff.
- a reinforcement of the school's messages about drugs.
- a model for future work by school staff.
- community links.
- an opportunity for students to prepare for and look after a visitor.

Step five:
Content of the curriculum

Target: Production of a drug education curriculum framework for the whole school.

How to go about it:

☐ Consult with teachers responsible for drug education in all parts of the school.

☐ Study National Curriculum documents.

☐ Consult outside experts.

☐ Examine teaching materials from a wide variety of sources.

The curriculum needs to be planned carefully so as to build on previous learning as the student progresses through the school.

'*All young people must be taught basic facts about drug misuse and related aspects of preventive health education.*' Drug Misuse and the Young: a guide for the education service.

The Order prescribes the following aspects of drug education for study in secondary schools:

Key Stage Three: Life and Living Processes

Pupils should be taught:

☐ how smoking affects breathing (lung structure and gas exchange).

☐ that the body's natural defences may be enhanced by immunisation and medicines.

☐ that the abuse of alcohol, solvents and other drugs affects health.

Key Stage Four: Life and Living Processes

Pupils should be taught:

☐ the effects of solvents, tobacco and other drugs on body functions.

The National Curriculum Guidance on drug education

The National Curriculum Council's *Curriculum Guidance 5: Health Education* recommends that in secondary schools students should:

Key Stage Three: Substance Use and Misuse

☐ Recognise personal responsibility for decisions about substance use.

☐ Know the basic facts about substances, including their effects and relevant legislation.

☐ Be aware of myths, misconceptions and stereotypes linked with substance use.

☐ Develop appropriate techniques for coping with situations in which substance use occurs.

Key Stage Four: Substance Use and Misuse

☐ Explore the historical, cultural, political, social and economic factors relating to the production, distribution and use of drugs worldwide.

☐ Understand that Britain is a drug using society, and recognise the different patterns of use and their effects, such as the transmission of HIV infection through shared needles, and the detrimental effect on the fetus of all types of drug use.

☐ Recognise that individuals are responsible for choices they make about drug use.

☐ Be able to analyse safe levels of intake; for instance, tobacco use is never safe, limited use of alcohol may be.

☐ Discuss the role of the media in influencing attitudes towards drugs, particularly smoking and alcohol.

☐ Be able to communicate effectively and confidently with those who administer medication.

'Research has shown that well planned health education can bring about positive changes which are demonstrated in responsible attitudes and behaviour.' **Curriculum Guidance 5.**

Topics for a secondary school drug education programme

'The acquisition of knowledge, understanding and skills which enable pupils to consider the effects of substances such as tobacco, alcohol and other drugs on themselves and others and to make informed and healthy decisions about the use of such substances...' Curriculum Guidance 5.

- What is a drug?
- Use of drugs
- Information about particular drugs
- What drugs look like
- How drugs are taken
- Effects of drugs, physical and psychological
- Where to go for help with problem drug use
- Why people take drugs
- Smoking education
- Influences on drug use
- Use of medicines
- Alcohol education
- Substances and safety education
- History of drugs and medicines
- Exploring attitudes and values about drugs and drug issues
- Development of self-esteem

- Development of skills such as assertiveness and decision making
- Stereotypes and prejudice
- Risk taking
- Drugs and HIV/AIDS
- Peer pressure
- Consequences of drug use
- Stress management
- Advertising and the media
- Problems, issues and situations: what would you do if...?
- Drugs and sport
- Myths and misconceptions
- Cultural influences
- Political, social and economic factors of production and distribution
- Choice and problem solving
- Safe and unsafe use
- Drugs and legislation

Drug education: the acrostic

D rugs play an important part in all our lives.

R esponsibility for drug education is shared between home, school and community.

U nderstanding about drugs is vital, since we live in a drug orientated society.

G reat emphasis should be placed on the development of skills.

E xploration of attitudes and values is a crucial component of drug education.

D rugs can have different effects at different times.

U sers' personalities and circumstances influence the effects of the drugs they take.

C ommunity issues and concerns should be taken into consideration when planning drug education.

A lcohol is a drug, and students should be taught to use it wisely,

T he development of self-esteem is an important factor in the prevention of drug misuse.

I nformed choice depends on knowledge, skills, values and attitudes.

O nly a whole school policy will guarantee a consistent approach.

N o one can solve their problems or create lasting happiness by taking drugs.

(handwritten notes: 0800 77 66 00 / 0800 567 123)

ADFAM National
(family support and self-help)
5th floor, Epworth House
25 City Road
London EC1Y 1AA
telephone 0171-638 3700

Alcohol Concern
Waterbridge House
32–36 Loman Street
London SE1 0EE
telephone 0171-928 7377

ASH (Action on Smoking and Health)
109 Gloucester Place
London W1H 4EJ
telephone 0171-935 3519

Educational Television Company
PO Box 100
Warwick CV34 6TZ
telephone 01926 433333

Health Publications Unit
(free leaflets etc.)
DSS Distribution Centre
Heywood Stores
Manchester Road
Heywood
Lancashire OL10 2PZ
telephone 0800 555 777 (free)

Doping Control Unit
The Sports Council
Walkden House
3–10 Melton Street
London NW1 2EB
telephone 0171-383 5667

Health Education Authority
Hamilton House
Mabledon Place
London WC1H 9TX
telephone 0171-383 3833

Health Wise
9 Slater Street
Liverpool L1 4BW
telephone 0151-707 2262

Institute for the Study of Drug
Dependence
Waterbridge House
32–36 Loman Street
London SE1 0EE
telephone 0171-928 1211
(publications)

Narcotics Anonymous
UK Service Office
PO Box 1980
London N19 3LS
telephone 0171-281 9933 (recording
about local meetings)
helpline 0171-498 9005
office 0171-272 9040

(handwritten note: drug awareness)

National AIDS Helpline
0800 567 123 (free)

National Alcohol Helpline
0171-332 0202

Release
(legal and welfare problems)
388 Old Street
London EC1V 9LT
telephone 0171-729 9904
emergency helpline 0171-603 8654

Re-Solv
(solvent misuse problems)
30a High Street
Stone
Staffordshire ST15 8AW
telephone 01785 817885

Scottish Drugs Forum
5 Oswald Street
Glasgow G1 4QR
telephone 0141-221 1175

Standing Council on Drug Abuse
(SCODA)
Waterbridge House
32-6 Loman Street
London SE1 0EE
telephone 0171-928 9500

TACADE
1 Hulme Place
The Crescent
Salford
Greater Manchester M5 4QA
telephone 0161-745 8925

Welsh Office Drugs Unit
Crown Building
Cathays Park
Cardiff CF1 3NQ
telephone 01222 825111

Basic Facts leaflet series: *AIDS/HIV, Alcohol, Drugs 1, Drugs 2, Smoking, Solvents*, TACADE updated 1994.

Curriculum Guidance 5: Health Education, National Curriculum Council 1990.

Drug Education in Schools: the need for a new impetus, a report by the Advisory Council on the Misuse of Drugs, HMSO 1993.

Drug Misuse and the Young: a guide for the education service, Department of Education 1992.

Drug Prevention and Schools, Circular 4/95, Department for Education 1994.

Drugs: a family matter (video training resource for parents), Department of Health 1992.

Raising the Issues: A Cross Curricular Approach to Drug Education, TACADE 1989.

Skills for Adolescence (Key Stages 2 and 3), TACADE 1986.

Skills for Life : a whole School approach to personal and social development at Key Stages 3 and 4, TACADE 1994.

Channel 4 Schools, *Off Limits: talking about drugs* (video, teacher's guide and information pack), Educational Television Company 1994.

Colin Chapman, *Drugs Issues for Schools: discussion document and background information*, Institute for the Study of Drug Dependence 1992.

Julian Cohen and James Kay, *Don't Panic: responding to incidents of young people's drug use*, Health Wise 1992.

Vivienne Evans, Bill Rice and Jeff Lee, *Think! Inform! Decide! a pack of 64 cards for discussion*, TACADE 1989.

Home Office, *Tackling Drugs Together: a consultation document on a strategy for England*, HMSO 1994.

Martin Plant, *Drugs in Perspective*, Hodder & Stoughton 1987.

Re-Solv, educational advisers TACADE, *'Chicken': A story about solvent misuse* (video and follow up materials), Prism Pictures.

Mike Ward and Bill Rice, *Taking Drugs, Taking Part: a resource concerning drugs and sport*, TACADE 1989.

Related titles from Daniels Publishing

Understanding Drugs 2nd edition
Ian Harvey
ISBN 1 85467 184 7

Peer-Led Drug Education
Barbara Jack and Ian Clements
ISBN 1 85467 225 8

Solvents, Drugs and Young People: a cross-curricular approach
Richard Ives and Barbara Wyvill
ISBN 1 85467 181 2

Ecstasy and Drug Use: learning activities
Julian Cohen
ISBN 1 85467 246 0

AIDSFacts 4th edition
Ian Harvey and Dr Michael Reiss
ISBN 1 85467 262 2

AlcoholFacts A and B
Dr Gerald Beales
ISBNs 1 85467 232 0 and 1 85467 233 9

SmokingFacts A and B
Dr Gerald Beales
ISBNs 1 85467 247 9 and 1 85467 221 5

Give Up Smoking for Good
Lee Adams and Mary Tidyman
ISBN 1 85467 254 1

Raising Self Esteem: 50 activities
Murray White
ISBN 1 85467 231 2

Self Esteem: its meaning and value in schools A and B
Murray White
ISBNs 1 85467 253 3 and 1 85467 263 0

Daniels Publishing resource packs are:

✔ **Fully photocopiable**

✔ **Ready for use**

✔ **Flexible**

✔ **Clearly designed**

✔ **Tried and tested**

✔ **Cost-effective**

The Quick Guide series from Daniels Publishing

Quick Guides are up to date, stimulating and readable A5 books, packed with essential information and key facts on important issues in education

Health education

Alcohol: A Quick Guide
Dr Gerald Beales
ISBN 1 85467 300 9

Drugs Education for children aged 4–11: A Quick Guide 2nd edition
Janice Slough
ISBN 1 85467 326 2

Drugs Education for children aged 11–18: A Quick Guide 2nd edition
Janice Slough
ISBN 1 85467 324 6

Eating Disorders: A Quick Guide
Dr Dee Dawson
ISBN 1 85467 321 1

Sex Education: A Quick Guide for Teachers
Dr Michael Kirby
ISBN 1 85467 228 2

Sex Education for children aged 4–11: A Quick Guide for parents and carers
Janice Slough
ISBN 1 85467 312 2

Sex Education for children aged 11–18: A Quick Guide for parents and carers
Janice Slough
ISBN 1 85467 313 0

Smoking Issues: A Quick Guide
Paul Hooper
ISBN 1 85467 309 2

Class and school management

Bullying: A Quick Guide 2nd edition
Dr Carrie Herbert
ISBN 1 85467 323 8

Equal Opportunities: A Quick Guide
Gwyneth Hughes & Wendy Smith
ISBN 1 85467 303 3

Governor Training: A Quick Guide
Michael Booker
ISBN 1 85467 320 3

Grief, Loss and Bereavement: A Quick Guide 2nd edition
Penny Casdagli & Francis Gobey
ISBN 1 85467 325 4

Primary School Inspections: A Quick Guide
Malcolm Massey and David Lee
ISBN 1 85467 308 4

Organising Conferences and Events: A Quick Guide
David Napier
ISBN 1 85467 314 9

Safety on Educational Visits: A Quick Guide
Michael Evans
ISBN 1 85467 306 8

Truancy: A Quick Guide
John Jones
ISBN 1 85467 319 X

Working in Groups: A Quick Guide
Pauline Maskell
ISBN 1 85467 304 1

Working with Parents: A Quick Guide
Dr Michael Kirby
ISBN 1 85467 315 7

Career enhancement

Assertiveness: A Quick Guide
Chrissie Hawkes-Whitehead
ISBN 1 85467 305 X

Counselling: A Quick Guide
Chrissie Hawkes-Whitehead and Cherry Eales
ISBN 1 85467 302 5

Problem People and How to Handle Them: A Quick Guide
Ursula Markham
ISBN 1 85467 317 3

Stress Management: A Quick Guide
Stephen Palmer and Lynda Strickland
ISBN 1 85467 316 5

For further information

For further details of any of our publications mentioned in this Quick Guide, please fill in and post this form (or a photocopy) to:

Daniels Publishing
38 Cambridge Place   Tel: 01223 467144
Cambridge CB2 1NS   Fax: 01223 467145

Name..

Job Title ....

Organisation..

Address ....

....

Postcode ....

Tel No..

Fax No. ....

☐ Please send me details of the following publications:

☐ Please keep me informed of forthcoming Quick Guides and other Health Education Resources from Daniels Publishing

Have you ordered from us before? ☐ No ☐ Yes: account no..........

Drug Education, ages 11–18: a quick guide